A New True Book

BLIZZARDS

By Arlene Erlbach

Consultants:

Paul Hoban, Meteorologist

David W. Phillips, Climatologiste principal,
Environment Canada

ℚℙ CHILDRENS PRESS ®
CHICAGO

The Chicago blizzard of 1979

PHOTO CREDITS
AP/Wide World Photos–32, 41
Ivy Images–35, 44
PhotoEdit–© Richard Hutchings, 4 (top);
© Myrleen Ferguson, 22 (left); © David
Young-Wolff, 34
Photri–© Photri, 10, 15; © T. Wachs, 38
Root Resources–© Kohout Productions,
Cover
Tom Stack & Associates–© Gary Milburn,
2; © Spencer Swanger, 20; © Robert
Winslow, 28; © Tom Stack, 37
SuperStock International, Inc.–© August
Upitis, 8; © Holton Collection, 30 (right)
Tony Stone Images–© Edward Lee, 6
Unicorn Stock Photos–© Gerry
Schnieders, 13; © Kathi Corder, 16; © Jay
Foreman, 33; © Joel Dexter, 43
Valan–© J.R. Page, 19; © Francis Lépine,
22 (right); © Jean Bruneau, 24; © Phil
Norton, 29; © Kennon Cooke, 30 (left);
© M. Julien, 42
Visuals Unlimited–© Richard Thom, 4
(bottom); © Kim Francisco, 7; © Linda H.
Hopson, 14; © Glenn Oliver, 26 (left);
© SIU, 26 (right); © Mark E. Gibson, 36
COVER: Shoveling out!

Project Editor: Fran Dyra
Design: Margrit Fiddle
Photo Research: Feldman & Associates, Inc.

*In memory of my mother,
Lillian Faverman, who walked
me through many snowstorms*

Library of Congress Cataloging-in-Publication Data

Erlbach, Arlene.
  Blizzards / by Arlene Erlbach.
    p.   cm.–(A New true book)
  Includes index.
  ISBN 0-516-01073-5
  1.   Blizzards–Juvenile literature.   2.   Blizzards–
United States–Juvenile literature.   3.   Winter storms–
Juvenile literature.   4.   Winter storms–United States–
Juvenile literature.   [1.   Blizzards.   2.   Weather.]
I. Title. II. Series.
QC926.37.E75 1995   94-36339
551.55'5–dc20   CIP
                                           AC

TABLE OF CONTENTS

WIND AND SNOW

Most people enjoy snow once in a while. We can go sledding or skiing. We can make snow people and build snow forts. And everything looks prettier covered with snow.

But some snowstorms have powerful winds and extreme cold. This kind of snowstorm is called a blizzard. Blizzards are

Opposite page: For many people, snow means fun and beauty.

Heavy snow makes driving difficult and dangerous.

usually dangerous and no fun at all.

During a blizzard, blowing snow makes it hard to see. Drivers and pedestrians may have accidents.

Digging out after a blizzard in Alaska

Snow piles up in drifts. It blocks roads. Trains, buses, and cars cannot move. Drifting snow also piles up on roofs. The weight of the snow may make a roof collapse.

7

Too much ice and snow damage trees and power lines.

A blizzard's strong winds can blow down power lines. Then people have no electricity or phones. Blizzards can cause millions of dollars in property damage. And sometimes lives are lost.

WHERE AND WHEN DO BLIZZARDS HAPPEN?

Most blizzards occur in Canada, Russia, or the north-central or northeastern parts of the United States. They usually happen during December, January, or February.

Fortunately, blizzards are not a common type of snowstorm. In North America, we get from one

Pedestrians are in danger when they are walking in heavy snow and high winds. It is hard to see, and cars or buses may slide into them while trying to stop at slippery corners.

to seven blizzards each year. But when a blizzard hits, people must take precautions. Even a snowstorm with near-blizzard conditions is dangerous.

WHAT MAKES A SNOWSTORM?

Precipitation is water that falls from clouds. It may fall as rain, sleet, hail, or snow.

Two important elements are needed for clouds to develop–moisture and sunlight.

When the sun warms the Earth's air, the air rises. The rising air carries a gas called water vapor. Water vapor contains millions and millions of water molecules.

The sun warms the Earth's oceans, lakes, and rivers. The air that rises from these bodies of water carries lots of water vapor.

As the warmed air rises, the water vapor condenses. This means that the water molecules move closer together and form tiny water droplets. As the water droplets rise, they form clouds.

High above the Earth, it is very cold. So the water droplets freeze and turn

A snowstorm
in Iowa

into ice crystals. Clouds
contain billions of ice
crystals.

The cloud's ice crystals
bump into each other and
form snowflakes. Finally, the
snowflakes become too big
and heavy to stay inside
the cloud. They drop out
and fall toward the Earth. **13**

If the air temperature near the ground is above freezing— 32 degrees Fahrenheit (0 degrees Celsius)—the snow melts. It falls to Earth as rain. But if the air temperature is below freezing, the snow remains snow as it falls to the ground.

People in the north are always prepared for heavy snow.

FLURRIES, SQUALLS, AND BLIZZARDS

Sometimes, snow falls lightly. It doesn't pile up. This type of snowfall is called a snow flurry. Usually, snow flurries do not last very long.

Big, wet snowflakes falling in a flurry

Sometimes we get a heavy snowfall that lasts for only a short time. Wind blows and snow piles up. This is called a snow squall.

For a snowstorm to be called a blizzard, it must have high winds as well as heavy snow.

When a blizzard happens, battering winds blow at 35 miles (56 kilometers) an hour or more. Heavy snow falls for hours.

WARM FRONTS AND COLD FRONTS

In a blizzard, two things occur at once—snow and strong winds. These two things can happen when cold air and warm air meet. The line where they meet is called a front.

Air travels in huge masses. An air mass may cover hundreds or thousands of miles or kilometers.

An air mass contains warm air or cold air—never both. All the air in an air mass is about the same temperature.

Warm air masses and cold air masses do not mix. Instead, one of the air masses pushes the other one.

When a warm air mass pushes a cold air mass, a warm front occurs. When a cold air mass pushes a warm air mass, a cold front results. Cold fronts can cause snowstorms.

These dark gray clouds are heavy with moisture
that may fall as rain or snow.

At the cold front, the warm air mass rises. The warm, rising air causes clouds to develop rapidly. These clouds are called stratus clouds. They stretch across the sky like a big gray blanket.

Blowing winds chill the winter air.

The rising movement of
the air also causes winds.
As the warm air rises, the
cooler air moves in to
replace it. This moving air
is called wind.

When the stratus clouds
are thick and heavy

enough, snow falls from them. The blowing winds chill the air. Then we have a snowstorm.

If the winds blow at 35 miles (56 kilometers) per hour or more, the snowstorm becomes a blizzard. The winds blow the snow and whip it around, making it difficult for people to see. This, combined with something called windchill temperature, makes a blizzard very hazardous.

On a summer day, the cooling effect of wind is welcome (left), but in the winter, windchill can make it dangerously cold.

WINDCHILL

Windchill is the cold you feel when the wind blows. On a hot day, wind can make you feel cooler and refreshed. On a winter day, the wind can make you feel colder and more uncomfortable.

Blowing winds make air feel colder than the thermometer says it is. Let's say that the air temperature is 30°F (-1°C)– a little below freezing. And let's say the wind is blowing at 40 miles (64 kilometers) per hour. Now the air feels as cold as it would if the temperature were really -5°F (-21°C). So the windchill temperature is -5°F (-21°C).

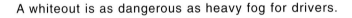

A whiteout is as dangerous as heavy fog for drivers.

BLIZZARD HAZARDS

The heavy, blowing snow of a blizzard makes it difficult to see. This condition is called whiteout. People can become lost and freeze to death in a whiteout. Even crossing streets can be dangerous.

Another danger during a blizzard is hypothermia. In hypothermia, a person's body temperature drops because of the extremely cold air. The heart rate slows, and the victim feels drowsy. Sometimes, people with hypothermia freeze to death.

The bitter cold of a blizzard can also cause

frostbite. This happens when skin is exposed to extremely cold air. The exposed skin freezes. Severe frostbite may cause permanent damage to fingers, toes, or ears.

In frostbite, white patches (left) or red areas (right) appear on the damaged skin.

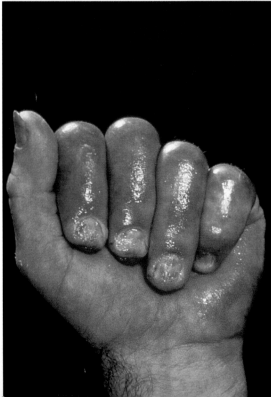

BLIZZARDS AND OTHER WEATHER CONDITIONS

A blizzard can cause other dangerous weather conditions.

For example, a blizzard may cause an avalanche. A blizzard's heavy snow and fierce winds may disturb the layers of snow lying on a mountainside. Then the snow rushes down the mountainside,

After an avalanche, rescue workers probe the deep snow with poles, looking for buried people.

crushing everything in its path. The snow crushes houses and sometimes buries people. If the people are not rescued in time, they usually die from hypothermia.

Blizzards can also cause floods. When the Earth warms in the springtime,

When heavy snows melt in the spring, the water runs into rivers and streams, contributing to flooding.

the deep snow melts. The meltwater runs into streams and rivers. The extra water causes them to overflow and flood the land.

In northern cities like Minneapolis and Chicago, people are used to heavy snow. Northern towns have snowplows ready to clean

Snowplows (left) go to work after a blizzard. Snowmobiles (right) help people travel in snow country.

their streets. Houses there are built to withstand cold weather. Some people own snowblowers and some have snowmobiles. People wear heavy coats, hats, gloves, and boots.

For these people, a blizzard is annoying. But it

is usually only an inconvenience, not a disaster.

But sometimes a blizzard or severe snowstorm occurs in an area where people are not accustomed to snow. People are unprepared. This makes any snowstorm very dangerous.

While blizzards are fairly unusual events, precipitation during the winter is common. And some of that winter weather can be almost as dangerous as a blizzard.

OTHER WINTER STORMS

Winter precipitation often includes sleet and freezing rain. Sleet is formed when snow falls from a cloud, melts into rain, and freezes again. The tiny ice pellets then fall as sleet.

Freezing rain forms when rain hits very cold ground and turns into ice. This makes streets slippery for pedestrians and drivers. When lots of freezing rain falls, we have an ice storm. Ice storms can be very beautiful–but dangerous.

Ice storms coat trees with layers of ice. The scene is beautiful, but the weight of the ice often causes branches to break.

PREDICTING BLIZZARDS AND WINTER STORMS

Meteorologists are scientists who study weather conditions. They tell us what to expect. They can predict severe winter weather.

TV weather reporters use maps to show weather conditions throughout the country.

This TV weather picture shows clouds moving across eastern North America.

Meteorologists have many tools to help them make predictions. They use satellites that take pictures from high above the Earth. They study the pictures to watch for approaching storms.

Meteorologists use radar

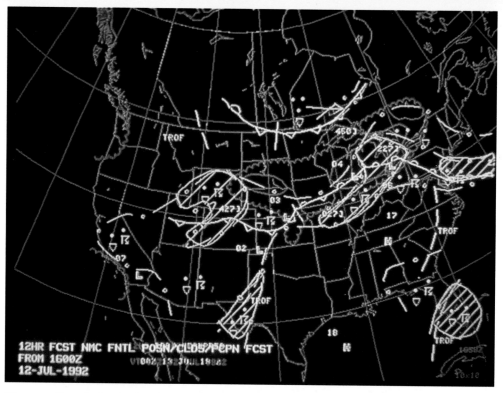

The weather information from satellites is shown on a screen. Can you find your state or province on this map?

too. The radar shows precipitation such as freezing rain, sleet, or snow.

Sometimes, blizzards and heavy snowstorms are difficult to predict. Weather conditions change quickly.

Clouds may move faster or slower than expected. A storm that was forecast may not occur. Or a weather report may predict light snow, and the next morning we might wake up to a howling blizzard.

WINTER STORM WARNINGS

Weather bureaus issue watches and warnings to radio and TV stations and newspapers when a winter storm may occur. It is important to know what these warnings mean.

Winter storm watch: Heavy snow and ice are possible within 48 hours.

Opposite page: After a snowstorm the scene can be beautiful, with a pure white blanket covering everything.

Winter storm warning:
Heavy snow will occur
soon–or has already
begun. Stay indoors.

Heavy snow warning:
More than 6 inches (15
centimeters) of snow will
fall within the next 24
hours.

Blizzard warning:
Heavy snow will fall,
accompanied by winds of
35 miles (56 kilometers)
per hour or more.

The effects of a heavy snowfall can be miserable
for people trying to get around.

Severe blizzard warning:
Heavy snow will fall and
winds will reach 45 miles
(72 kilometers) per hour or
more. Temperatures may fall
to -10°F (-23°C) or below.

41

During a blizzard or any
severe winter storm, stay
indoors. Do not travel far
from home. If you must go
out, bundle up. Wear
several layers of clothing.
Cover your head. Protect
your face with a scarf or

Warm clothing worn in layers protects us from the wind and cold.

ski mask. Be sure to wear boots and mittens or gloves.

Everyone should pay attention to weather warnings and watches. They tell us what kind of weather we can expect. And they are usually right.

MAJOR WINTER STORMS IN NORTH AMERICA

YEAR	LOCATION	DAMAGE & DEATHS
1888	Eastern U.S.	Blizzard, 24 inches (61cm) of snow. 400 deaths.
1900	Kansas City to New York	Blizzard, over 1-1/2 feet (46 cm) in some areas. Five feet (152 cm) in Adirondack Mountain region.
1922	Washington, D.C.	Heavy snowstorm 19 inches (48 cm). Especially hazardous because it fell in an area unaccustomed to heavy snowfall.
1940	Midwestern States and Canada to Louisiana	Blizzard, more than 100 deaths.
1940	Second blizzard from Canada to U.S.	Blizzard, more than 60 deaths.
1947	New York	Heavy snowstorm, 36 inches (91 cm). More than 70 deaths.
1947	Regina, Canada	A blizzard raged for ten days.
1967	Chicago	Heavy snowstorm, 19 inches (48 cm) in 24 hours. Storm did not qualify as blizzard.
1971	Montreal, Canada	Almost 2 feet (61 cm) of snow, and winds 68 mph (109 kph). Electricity out for almost a week in many homes.
1978	Ohio	Entire state buried due to snowstorms and blizzards. Over 60 deaths.
1978	New England	Four days of heavy snow and blizzards. More than 20 deaths.
1978	New York	Heavy snowstorm, almost 17 inches (43 cm).
1982	Prince Edward Island, Canada	Winds of almost 50 mph (80 kph) and 2 feet (61 cm) of snow. Islanders marooned for five days.
1986	Winnipeg, Canada	55 mph (89 kph) winds and a foot (30 cm) of snow. Clean up cost three million dollars.
1993	Florida, South Carolina, Georgia, North Carolina, Virginia, West Virginia, Pennsylvania, New York, Alabama, Tennessee, Kentucky, Maryland, Maine	Heavy snowstorms and blizzards over a four day period. Over 200 related deaths. Called the "storm of the century."

MAJOR WINTER STORMS WORLDWIDE

YEAR	LOCATION	DAMAGE & DEATHS
1925	Korea	Heavy snow, 200 deaths.
1928	Turkey	Blizzard with temperatures −49°F (−56°C), 70 deaths
1931	Japan	30 deaths. Storm derailed train and tore roofs off 1,000 houses.
1936	Bulgaria	100 deaths.
1937	Western Balkans	57 deaths.
1942 and 1943	Stalingrad, Russia	Severe cold and heavy snowfall killed over 250,000 German soldiers.
1943	Europe	Blizzards and severe cold killed thousands.
1949	Tehran, Iran	Heavy snow left 73,000 homeless.
1956	Western Europe	Blizzard caused 1,000 deaths.
1978	Scotland	Blizzard lasted for fifty hours between January 27 and 29.
1982	South Wales and western England	Blizzard made most roads impassable.
1990	Scotland and Northern Ireland	Blizzards and winds of over 70 mph (113 kph).
1992	Turkey	Blizzard blocked roads. About 140 deaths caused by related avalanche.

WORDS YOU SHOULD KNOW

avalanche (AV • uh • lanch)–a large mass of snow that suddenly slides down a mountain

condense (kun • DENSE)–to change from a gas to a liquid

extreme (ex • TREEM)–to a great degree; intense

forecast (FOR • kast)–predicted to happen

hazardous (HAZ • er • duss)–dangerous; unsafe

hypothermia (hi • puh • THERM • ee • ya)–very low body temperature caused by severe cold

ice crystals (ICE KRISS • tilz)–small particles of ice found in clouds

inconvenience (in • kun • VEEN • yence)–trouble; a burden

ingredients (in • GREED • ee • ents)–parts that go into a mixture

meteorologist (me • tee • or • AHL • uh • jist)–a scientist who studies the weather

moisture (MOYS • chur)–dampness; wetness

molecule (MAHL • ih • kyool)–the smallest particle of a substance that can exist and still keep its chemical form

pedestrians (peh • DESS • tree • inz)–people who are walking along sidewalks or crossing streets

precautions (pri • KAW • shunz)–protection; steps taken to keep someone or something safe

precipitation (prih • sih • pih • TAY • shun)–water that falls from clouds in the form of rain, sleet, hail, or snow

predict (prih • DIKT)–to tell ahead of time

radar (RAY • dahr)–a device that finds objects by bouncing radio waves off them

satellite (SAT • ih • lite)–an artificial body that revolves around Earth high above the surface and contains instruments to measure conditions on Earth

severe (sih • VEER)–harsh; cruel

squall (SKWAWL)–a short, severe storm

stratus cloud (STRAT • us KLOUD)–a low, solid, gray cloud that covers a large area

water vapor (WAW • ter VAY • per)–water that has been turned into a gas by heating

whiteout (WITE • out)–conditions of very low visibility due to blowing snow

INDEX

About the Author

Arlene Erlbach has written twenty-three books for young people in many genres including fiction and nonfiction.

She has a master's degree in special education. In addition to being an author of children's books she is a learning disabilities teacher at Gray School in Chicago, Illinois. Arlene loves to encourage children to write and is in charge of her school's Young Authors program.